Marvel Studios' Thor: Ragnarok

Based on the Screenplay by
Eric Pearson, Craig Kyle, Christopher L. Yost
Story by Stan Lee, Larry Lieber, and Jack Kirby

Produced by Kevin Feige, p.g.a.
Directed by Taika Waititi

Level 3

Retold by Karen Holmes

Series Editors: Andy Hopkins and Jocelyn Potter

Pearson Education Limited

KAO Two

KAO Park, Harlow,

Essex, CM17 9NA, England

and Associated Companies throughout the world.

ISBN: 978-1-2923-4749-3

This edition first published by Pearson Education Ltd 2018

1 3 5 7 9 10 8 6 4 2

© 2021 MARVEL

The authors have asserted their moral rights in accordance
with the Copyright Designs and Patents Act 1988

Set in 9pt/14pt Xenois Slab Pro

Printed by Neografia, Slovakia

Published by Pearson Education Limited

For a complete list of the titles available in the Pearson English Readers series, visit
www.pearsonenglishreaders.com.
Alternatively, write to your local Pearson Education office or
to Pearson English Readers Marketing Department,
Pearson Education, KAO Two, KAO Park, Harlow, Essex, CM17 9NA

Contents

Who's Who?

Thor

Thor, the God of Thunder, is an Asgardian prince. His father, Odin, was King of Asgard and protector of the Nine Realms. Thor is brave, and his hammer—Mjolnir—gives him great fighting power. He often has problems with his brother, Loki.

Loki

Loki is Odin's younger son. He is not strong, like Thor, but he is smart. His power comes from his control of people's minds. They see what he wants them to see. He can change his appearance, and move at great speed.

Hela

Hela is Odin's oldest child. She is very dangerous, and more powerful when she is on Asgard. She wants to be Queen of Asgard and control the Nine Realms. Odin couldn't control her, so he put her in prison in another realm.

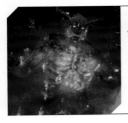

Surtur

Surtur was King of Muspelheim. He looks like a skeleton. The Eternal Flame makes him powerful. Many years ago, Odin won a war against him and took this flame. Now Surtur wants to find it again, and to destroy Asgard.

Heimdall

Heimdall is a brave Asgardian fighter. He can see and hear almost everything that happens in the Nine Realms. He usually guards the Rainbow Bridge and the Bifrost, and watches for enemy attacks on Asgard and other dangers.

Skurge

Skurge is an Asgardian soldier who has fought for his king and his people. Now, Loki has given him an important job; he controls the way to and from the Bifrost. From his guard post, Skurge must stop enemies arriving on Asgard.

Bruce Banner / Hulk

Banner is a very smart scientist from Earth. When he is angry, though, he becomes Hulk. Hulk is a big, green, dangerous fighter. Hulk crashed his spaceship on the planet Sakaar, and now he lives there. He is the Grandmaster's favorite fighter.

Scrapper 142

Scrapper 142 was one of a group of fighters called the Valkyries. She left Asgard after she and the other Valkyries lost a fight with Hela. Now she lives on Sakaar and works for the Grandmaster.

The Grandmaster

The Grandmaster is a strange man who controls the planet Sakaar. He loves to play games with weaker life forms, so he organizes big fights. The fighters are his prisoners. His people only love him because of these games.

Introduction

Odin's voice was very weak. "I failed you. Ragnarok has come!"

"No," Thor said quickly. "I've stopped Ragnarok. I killed Surtur."

"No. Ragnarok has already begun. I am dying and she is coming. I cannot keep her away."

"Father, who are you talking about?" Thor asked.

"The Goddess of Death," Odin replied. "Hela. My first-born child. Your sister."

When Thor, the God of Thunder, returns to Asgard, everything has changed. His father, Odin, has disappeared. The gatekeeper to the Bifrost, Heimdall, has also disappeared. And Thor's brother, Loki, is playing tricks again.

Thor and Loki find their father, but Odin has bad news for them. He is dying, and his death will open the gates of Asgard to their older sister, Hela. Hela wants the throne of Asgard. She also wants to control *all* the Nine Realms—and nothing will stop her.

Marvel Studios' Thor: Ragnarok was first shown in 2017. It followed two other movies about Thor and his family: *Marvel Studios' Thor* (2011) and *Marvel Studios' Thor: The Dark World* (2013). *Thor: Ragnarok* stars Chris Hemsworth as Thor, Tom Hiddleston as Loki, and Cate Blanchett as Hela. The movie was very successful. It is full of action and adventure, with some exciting fights between spaceships. It is also very funny!

Marvel is famous for its stories about powerful gods, and strange men and women from other worlds. Stories about Thor, Odin, and Loki were first told hundreds of years ago in the Scandinavian countries of northern Europe (Norway, Sweden, and Denmark). In these stories, Odin was the father of all the other gods.

In the Marvel stories, Odin is a wise god and King of Asgard. Asgard is one of a group of planets called the Nine Realms. Earth (also called Midgard) is another of these realms. The Bifrost is used to reach one realm from another in no time. If people want to reach the Bifrost from the palace of Asgard, they cross the Rainbow Bridge. The gatekeeper opens the entrance to the Bifrost with his sword, and people can then travel to other realms.

Odin's greatest enemy is Surtur, the King of Muspelheim. Many years ago, the two kings fought a war, and Odin won. He stole the Eternal Flame from Surtur. This flame made Surtur powerful—and now Surtur wants it back.

Odin was helped in his wars by women soldiers, the Valkyries. They flew through the air on white horses, and were very brave. Many of them died in a fight with Odin's daughter, Hela.

In *Thor: Ragnarok*, Thor is taken prisoner on the planet Sakaar. It is covered in trash. Sakaar is controlled by a strange and dangerous man, the Grandmaster. He likes to watch his prisoners fight—and die! Will he destroy Thor? Or can Thor escape and save Asgard? Can he find friends—old and new—to help him? Or is Ragnarok, the fall of Asgard, really coming?

Thor's Return to Asgard

In a room deep under the ground, Thor couldn't move any part of his body.

"I know what you're thinking," he said. "Thor's a prisoner—how did this happen? It's a long story, but I'm really very strong and very brave."

His hair and beard were long, and his clothes were dirty. He didn't look like the God of Thunder.

"I spent some time on Earth, and saved the planet a few times. Then I came to a path of death. The path brought me all the way here ..." He turned toward the center of the room. "And I met you."

A skeleton was sitting on a big rock throne. It was covered in flames and had sharp horns on its head.

"Thor, son of Odin," it said.

"Surtur, King of Muspelheim," Thor replied. "You're still alive! I thought my father killed you half a million years ago!"

"I cannot die until I destroy your home—Asgard."

"That's strange," Thor said. "I had these terrible dreams about Asgard in flames. And you, Surtur, were at the center of all of them."

"You have seen Ragnarok, the fall of Asgard. My time has come. I will put my crown into the Eternal Flame, and I will be powerful again. I will be as tall as a mountain! I will put my sword deep in Asgard's—"

"O.K.," Thor said slowly. "You're going to put your crown into the Eternal Flame. And you'll suddenly grow to the size of a house—"

"A mountain!" Surtur shouted angrily.

"Into the Eternal Flame that protects the Nine Realms? The flame that Odin has locked away on Asgard?"

Surtur gave a scary smile. "Odin is not on Asgard. And *you* left the throne with nobody to defend it."

This was news to Thor. Where *was* Odin? He continued, "O.K., so where is your crown?"

"*This* is my crown." Surtur pointed at the V-shaped horns on his head.

"Oh, that's a *crown*? I didn't realize," Thor said. "So, I'll knock that thing off your head. That will stop Ragnarok."

Surtur stood up and walked toward Thor. "You cannot stop it. Ragnarok has already begun. Everyone will suffer, everyone will burn. Why fight it?"

"Because that's what brave people do."

BOOM! Behind his back, Thor's hammer, Mjolnir, crashed through the wall into his hands. Thor broke free from the wall. He threw Mjolnir at Surtur and hit him in the face. The hammer immediately returned to Thor's hand.

Surtur sent a wall of fire toward the God of Thunder. Thor jumped high into the air, then he cut his enemy's head off his body. Thor picked up Surtur's crown of horns, and tied it to his back.

In the shadows, a big Fire Dragon freed itself from the wall. It ran

Surtur sent a wall of fire toward the God of Thunder.

toward Thor.

"This is too big to fight," Thor realized. "I need to return to Asgard—now!" He lifted Mjolnir above his head and called up to his friend on Asgard for help. "Heimdall, I need a fast exit. Heimdall?"

Heimdall was an Asgardian soldier who saw everything in the Nine Realms. He guarded the Rainbow Bridge and the Bifrost, and watched for attacks on Asgard.

There was no reply. Thor shouted again. "Heimdall, my clothes are in flames! Help me!"

The dragon opened its mouth, ready to attack Thor.

Thor looked up at the sky. "I need help—now!" he shouted.

His call wasn't answered.

The Rainbow Bridge ran from the palace in Asgard to Heimdall's golden-roofed guard post at the start of the Bifrost. The Bifrost joined Asgard to each of the Nine Realms. Usually, Heimdall and his special sword opened the entrance to the Bifrost—but Heimdall wasn't there.

Inside the guard post, another man—Skurge—was talking to two Asgardian women. "Heimdall was crazy," he told them. "With control of the Bifrost, I can take anything from the Nine Realms. This job can make you rich—and Heimdall lost it! I was given his job."

He picked up two guns. "I love these guns. I found them in a place called

Texas. I gave them names—Des and Troy. If you put the words together, their names make the word 'destroy'!"

Behind Skurge, a light came on at the center of the Bifrost controls.

"Is that important?" one of the women asked.

Skurge turned and noticed the Bifrost activity. He looked around for Heimdall's sword. It was lying in a corner of the room. He picked it up and put it into the controls. Suddenly, the Bifrost opened and Thor came in at top speed. The Fire Dragon followed, its mouth wide open. The Bifrost closed again and cut the dragon's head from its body.

The dragon's green blood poured down on Skurge and the two women. Its head moved slowly across the floor. The women screamed and ran out of the room.

Thor stood up and looked at Skurge. "Who are you?" he asked. "Where's Heimdall?"

"Nobody knows," Skurge said. "The gatekeeper didn't do his job, so Odin was angry with him. He wanted to punish him. But then Heimdall disappeared."

Thor moved toward the exit. He lifted Mjolnir and flew into the air.

"And so, smart Loki saved Asgard—but he gave his life for his home, his father, and the Nine Realms." The actor on the stage ended his speech.

A large crowd of Asgardians was enjoying the show. Seated on a great throne, Odin was enjoying it, too.

When the people in the crowd started talking, Odin turned angrily. Then suddenly, he looked very nervous. Thor was walking straight toward him. Everyone was talking about the God of Thunder's return ...

Thor lifted Surtur's skull. "Father," he said to Odin. "Do you know what this is?"

"The skull of Surtur?" Odin replied. "That's dangerous."

Thor passed the skull to a guard. "Lock it in a dark room so it doesn't destroy the planet." He continued: "I've had strange dreams. Every night, I see Asgard in flames ... Our enemies are planning to destroy us and you,

Odin, the protector of the Nine Realms, are watching a play!"

"That's just a silly dream ..." Odin started.

"Do I really have to do it?" Thor asked angrily.

"Do what?"

Thor threw his hammer, Mjolnir, far away. At the same time, he took Odin by the back of the neck and stood behind him. Odin's guards ran to help their king. Thor kicked them away.

Mjolnir stopped and flew back—toward Odin's head.

"Nothing will stop Mjolnir flying into my hand," Thor said. "Not even your face—*brother*!"

The hammer flew toward Odin's head. "O.K., O.K.!" he shouted. And then "Odin" disappeared and Loki stood in his place! It was one of Loki's tricks.

The Asgardians watched the brothers. Some of them were very angry with Loki.

Thor caught Mjolnir. "Where's Father?" he asked. He pressed his hammer onto Loki's chest.

"*Ow-ow-ow!*" Loki screamed. "You couldn't stay away from Asgard, could you? Everything was fine without you."

"Where's Father?" Thor repeated. "Did you kill him?"

"No! I know exactly where he is," Loki replied.

He pressed his hammer onto Loki's chest.

A Very Special Sister

Thor and Loki were standing on a sidewalk in New York City. They were wearing Earth clothes and Thor was carrying an umbrella. In front of them was a large building with a sign: Shady Acres. It was a home for old people.

"I left him here!" Loki said. "I promise."

"Here on the sidewalk? Or there, in that building—the building that those men are pulling down?" Thor pointed at Shady Acres.

"I didn't know!"

"I can't believe that you're alive," Thor said angrily. "I saw you die. I *cried* for you."

Suddenly, the sidewalk lit up under Loki's feet.

"What's this? What are you doing?" Thor shouted. Was this another of Loki's tricks?

"*I* didn't do that," Loki replied, surprised. Then he disappeared into a hole in the sidewalk. The hole closed again. In its place was a card with an address: 177A Bleecker Street.

Thor walked quickly to the address and knocked on the door. The door didn't open, but suddenly Thor was inside a dark house. A strange man was moving toward him. His feet weren't touching the floor.

Thor looked down at his hand. He was still carrying an umbrella and not his hammer, Mjolnir.

"Thor, son of Odin, God of Thunder," the man said. "You can put down the umbrella."

"Who are you?" Thor asked.

"My name is Dr. Stephen Strange, and I have some questions for you. I guard other realms from danger—danger from people like your brother Loki."

"He *is* dangerous," Thor agreed.

"So why did you bring him here?"

"We're looking for my father," Thor said.

"I will tell you where Odin is," Doctor Strange said. "Then, you must all return to Asgard."

"You know where my father is? Why didn't you call and tell me?"

"Do you have a telephone?" Doctor Strange asked.

"No," Thor replied. "Why not send an email?"

"Do you have a computer?" Doctor Strange asked.

"No. Why do I need a computer?" Thor really didn't understand the modern Earth world. "I want to take my father home," he said. "He can go back to Asgard now."

"Your father is in Norway," Doctor Strange said. "He is waiting for you."

A bright circle of light shone from Doctor Strange's hands, and a portal opened. Thor looked through it to a field of green grass.

"Don't forget your umbrella," Doctor Strange told him.

The umbrella flew into Thor's hand. "I need my brother," he said.

Doctor Strange waved his hands in the air.

Screaming loudly, Loki fell through a portal above them onto the floor. "I was falling ... for *thirty minutes!*" he said angrily.

"You can take him," Doctor Strange said. "Good luck."

"Who are you?" Loki asked angrily. He pulled out a knife.

"Loki, stop!" Thor said. He turned to Doctor Strange. "Thank you for your help."

"Goodbye," Doctor Strange said, and pushed Thor and Loki through the portal.

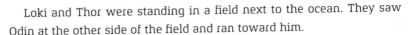

Loki and Thor were standing in a field next to the ocean. They saw Odin at the other side of the field and ran toward him.

"Father, it's us," Thor said.

"My sons, I've waited for you for a long time," the old man said sadly.

"We've come to take you home."

"Yes, I want to go home. Can you hear your mother's voice? She is calling me. Come and sit with me. I don't have much time." His voice was very weak. "I failed you. Ragnarok has come!"

"No," Thor said quickly. "I've *stopped* Ragnarok. I killed Surtur."

"No. Ragnarok has already begun. I am dying and *she* is coming. I cannot keep her away."

"Father, who are you talking about?" Thor asked.

"The Goddess of Death," Odin replied. "Hela. My first-born child. Your sister."

Thor was surprised. A sister? "What?"

"She was too powerful. I couldn't control her, so I locked her away in another realm. She stayed away because I was alive. But now my life has ended. She is already strong, but Asgard will make her stronger. She gets her power from our home ... Now she will return, and she will destroy everything."

"We can stop her together," Thor said.

There was a tear in the one eye that was left to Odin after an earlier fight. "No. I am dying," he said again. "You must fight her alone. I love you, my sons." He looked at the sun shining on the ocean. "Remember this place. It is home."

He slowly disappeared. Odin was dead.

The sky became darker and the wind grew stronger. There was thunder in the air. Thor turned to Loki. His eyes were very angry. "*You* did this!" he cried.

CRACK! A portal opened behind them, filled with green light. Suddenly, Thor and Loki were wearing their Asgardian clothes again, and Thor was now carrying his hammer, Mjolnir. He and Loki were dressed for a fight.

A frightening-looking woman came through the portal. She was tall and thin, and her eyes were very black. "So, he's gone? That's sad," she said. "I wanted to see him die."

"Are you Hela? I'm Thor, son of Odin," Thor greeted her.

Hela looked closely at him. "Really? You don't look like him," she said.

"Maybe we can come to an agreement about the throne of Asgard," Loki started.

Hela laughed. "You *sound* like him." She lifted a long, black sword. "Get down on your knees in front of your queen," she ordered both men.

"I don't think so," Thor said. He threw Mjolnir at her. Hela lifted her hand and the hammer stopped.

Thor was very surprised. He called for Mjolnir, but Hela held it.

"That's not possible," Thor said.

"Brother, you don't know what is possible." Hela broke Thor's hammer into a thousand pieces. Then she touched her head. Suddenly, she was wearing a black crown of sharp horns.

Loki looked up and shouted at the sky. "Take us back to Asgard!" he cried, afraid.

"No!" Thor shouted. He didn't want to take Hela home with them. She was more powerful there. But he was too late. Immediately, the Bifrost opened and covered all three of them.

Thor and Loki flew up toward Asgard, and Hela followed them.

Thor and Loki flew up toward Asgard, and Hela followed them.

Loki threw two long knives at his sister, but she flew straight through them. She knocked Loki out of the Bifrost. Next, Hela attacked Thor. He fought her, but she knocked him out of the Bifrost, too. He and Loki both disappeared.

On Asgard, Hela killed two guards, then walked slowly toward Skurge. He lifted his hands in fear. "Don't hurt me! I'm only the gatekeeper," he said.

She looked at him carefully. "You look like a smart guy. Do you want a job? Every great king has an assistant, somebody to kill people. I killed people for Odin. *You* can kill people for *me*."

Soon, Hela and Skurge were outside the palace. The people of Asgard were standing below them.

Hela lifted her arms and shouted, "I am Hela, Odin's first-born child. I am the Goddess of Death. My father is dead and the throne of Asgard belongs to me. Thor and Loki are dead, too. My father was weak. He only wanted to control the Nine Realms. But I want to control *everything* and *everyone*!"

Her guards moved closer to the Asgardians. Hela ordered the people, "Get down on your knees in front of me!"

A small group of Thor's friends and their soldiers prepared to attack her. "I don't know who you are," one of them shouted. "But stop now!"

"You don't know me?" Hela asked angrily. "I told you! Didn't you listen? Why aren't you happy to see me?"

The horns grew on her head again and she killed Thor's friends and the soldiers, one by one. Soon, they were all dead.

"Oh, I've missed these fights," Hela said happily. "Good soldiers died because they didn't accept me. They couldn't see the future. That's sad." She turned to Skurge. "Let's go and see my palace."

At the end of the Rainbow Bridge, a man was climbing toward the guard post. A cloth hid his face. He looked at the Bifrost's controls and picked up Heimdall's sword ...

A Prisoner on Sakaar

Thor was lying on his back on a pile of scrap. All around him was more scrap—pieces of old, broken spaceships. Above him, more metal was falling through black holes in the clouds. He looked across the ocean and saw a different kind of hole. It was very big and full of smoke and lightning.

There was a spaceship near the water. Next to it, a group of men were picking up scrap metal. *They're Scrappers*, Thor thought. Scrappers were dangerous people who sold trash. Sometimes they sold people, too.

One of them saw him. "Are you a fighter, or are you food?"

"I'm just passing through this place," Thor said. He reached for Mjolnir, but his hammer didn't come to him. It was destroyed by Hela.

"So you're food," the Scrapper said. He and his friends attacked Thor.

Thor fought hard, but they were too strong for him. They pushed him to the ground. Then, they tied him until he couldn't move. He was very angry, but without Mjolnir he couldn't fight the Scrappers.

Suddenly, another spaceship arrived and a woman stepped out of it. She was small, but she looked like a fighter. She wore black gloves. She wasn't afraid of the Scrappers.

"Wait!" she shouted. "If you want him, you must fight me first."

The Scrappers lifted their guns. "But we already have him," one of them said angrily.

"O.K., then *I'll* fight *you*." She hit her gloves together. Nothing happened. She hit her gloves together again and there was a loud noise. Guns came out of the sides of her spaceship. Soon the Scrappers were all dead on the ground.

"Thank you," Thor said.

The woman looked at him for a long time. Then she took a small metal disk and threw it onto Thor's neck. She pressed a control switch in her glove. Electricity filled Thor's body, and he screamed with pain.

The woman pulled Thor into her spaceship and put him into a small glass room. She spoke into her radio. "This is Scrapper 142. I want to see the boss. I have a special gift for him."

Thor opened his eyes. All of his body hurt. "Hey! Where are you taking me? Answer me! I am Thor, son of Odin. I must get back to Asgard."

"Sorry," Scrapper 142 said. She pressed the control switch again.

Thor screamed with pain and closed his eyes.

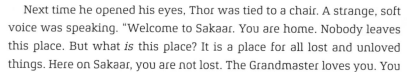

Next time he opened his eyes, Thor was tied to a chair. A strange, soft voice was speaking. "Welcome to Sakaar. You are home. Nobody leaves this place. But what *is* this place? It is a place for all lost and unloved things. Here on Sakaar, you are not lost. The Grandmaster loves you. You belong to him! You will meet the Grandmaster in five seconds."

The Grandmaster came toward Thor. He was a tall man in a long, shiny, golden coat. His hair was silver, and a blue line ran down from his mouth. His guard and Scrapper 142 were with him.

He looked at Thor. "He's wonderful," he said to Scrapper 142. "It is a 'he'?"

"Yes, it is a he," she replied.

"I love your visits, 142. You bring me the best stuff." He turned to Topaz, his guard. "What do I always say about Scrapper 142? She is the ... What's the word? It starts with a 'b.'"

"Trash," Topaz said, looking angrily at Scrapper 142.

"No, not trash. That doesn't start with a 'b.' No, 'best.' I was thinking about the word 'best.' Scrapper 142 brought me my wonderful champion, my best fighter. What have you brought today, 142? I want a closer look." He looked carefully at Thor, then turned to Topaz. "Pay this lady."

"Wait a minute. I'm not for sale," Thor said. He pushed hard against the chair and broke away from it.

"*Wow!*" the Grandmaster said. "He *is* a fighter."

Scrapper 142 pressed her control switch again. Electricity poured through Thor and he stopped moving.

"I'll take ten million units* for him," Scrapper 142 said. She turned toward the door.

"You'll pay for this!" Thor shouted.

"No," she said. "The *Grandmaster* paid *me*."

Thor pulled at the metal disk in his neck, but he couldn't get it off. The Grandmaster had a control switch, too. He used it and Thor screamed with pain.

"Who are you?" the Grandmaster asked.

"I am the God of Thunder!" Thor shouted.

"*Wow!* I didn't hear any thunder. I'll introduce myself. My name is the Grandmaster. We have great games here on Sakaar. People come from many different planets to fight my champion. And you are one of them, my friend. Isn't that exciting?"

* units: money, on Sakaar and many other planets

The Grandmaster came toward Thor.

"We're not friends, and I'm not interested in your games! I'm going back to Asgard!" Thor looked around. There was a group of well-dressed people standing near the Grandmaster. And one of them was ... Loki! He was wearing Sakaarian clothes.

"Loki? *Loki!* Come here!" Thor shouted.

Loki looked very worried when he saw Thor. He moved closer to his brother. "You're alive! What are you doing here?" he asked quietly.

"What am I doing?" Thor said. "I can't move out of this chair! Get me out of here."

"I can't," Loki said. "The Grandmaster is my friend—he likes me. The Bifrost brought me here weeks ago."

"*Weeks* ago?" Thor said. "I just arrived!"

Suddenly, the Grandmaster was standing next to them. "Time works differently here," he said. "Outside Sakaar, I'm a million years old. What are you two guys talking about? Loki, do you know this ... Lord of Thunder?"

"*God* of Thunder," Thor said angrily. "Loki, tell him."

"I've never met this man before in my life," Loki lied.

"He's my brother!" Thor shouted.

"Can he fight?" the Grandmaster asked Loki.

"He's O.K.," Loki said.

"Take this metal disk out of my neck and I'll show you," Thor said.

"Oh, you're brave!" the Grandmaster said. "O.K., you can fight my champion. If you win, you can go home."

Some guards took Thor into a room and shut the door. He tried to open it, but it didn't move.

He heard a slow, calm voice behind him. "Hey! Stay calm, man! Yes, I'm the pile of rocks that's waving at you. My name is Korg. I'm the boss in this prison. I'm made of rocks, but don't be afraid of me. And this is my very good friend, Miek. He's from another planet." He pointed at a small animal with sharp knives for fingers.

Thor looked at the strange rock man. "You're a Kronan, aren't you? Why are you here?"

"I tried to start a revolution on my planet, but I forgot to tell people. Nobody joined me, except my mom and her boyfriend. My government sent me here to punish me. But I'm organizing another revolution to escape from here. Are you interested?"

"Has anybody here fought the Grandmaster's champion?" Thor asked.

"Doug has," Korg said. He looked around. There was a body lying on the ground. "Oh, Doug's dead. I forgot. Everyone dies when they fight the Grandmaster's champion."

"Have *you* fought him?" Thor asked.

"No. I only do the smaller fights. They get the crowd excited before the main fight. You're not going to fight the champion, are you?"

"Yes, I am. I'll fight him and I'll win. Then I'll get out of here."

Korg laughed. "Doug said that, too. See you later, new Doug."

Korg and Miek walked away.

On Asgard, Hela and Skurge were in a room deep under the palace.

"Here are Odin's most important prizes," Skurge said.

Hela laughed. "Most of these things aren't real," she said. She picked up Surtur's skull. "This isn't very big."

She noticed the Tesseract, a box made of very hard glass. A bright light shone inside the glass. Something powerful was inside it.

"That's not bad," Hela said.

Then she saw something more interesting.

"The Eternal Flame," Hela said quietly. She put her hand into it, and her fingers held its flames. "Do you want to see what true power really looks like?" she asked Skurge. She jumped down into a dark place under the ground, full of skeletons. "These were my soldiers," she said softly. Then, she saw a skeleton of a very big wolf. "Fenris! My love! What have they done to you? With the Eternal Flame, you will live again!"

The fire from the Eternal Flame moved out from Hela's fingers and covered her soldiers and Fenris. Immediately, they all came to life again, and they started to move.

"I've missed you. I've missed you all," Hela said.

Skurge looked very worried.

Thor Meets an Old Friend

The Grandmaster's guards took Thor, Korg, and some other fighters from their room to a large outdoor theater. It was a place where the Sakaarians watched games and fights.

Thor noticed Scrapper 142. "Do you see her?" he asked Korg. "She put me in here."

"Yes," Korg said. "She's strong. Those Asgardians are dangerous. They're difficult to kill."

"She's Asgardian?" Thor ran to Scrapper 142. "Hey!"

She lifted the control switch in her hand.

"Do *not* use that thing," Thor said. "I only want to talk to you. Asgard is in danger." He saw a small, dark picture on her arm. It was burned into her skin. He knew those pictures ... "You're a Valkyrie!" The Valkyries were famous Asgardian fighters.

"I wanted to be a Valkyrie when I was a boy," Thor continued. "But all the Valkyries were women. I don't have a problem with women, Valkyrie. I *love* women! Sometimes I love them too much—"

"Have you finished?" Valkyrie asked angrily.

One of the guards came to him. "It's time to go."

"Please, help me," Thor said to Valkyrie.

She turned away from him. "Goodbye."

"You *must* help me!" Thor shouted. "What's your problem? Are you afraid? The Valkyries promised to protect the throne of Asgard."

"Listen carefully," Valkyrie said. "This is *Sakaar*, not *Asgard*. And I'm a *Scrapper*, not a *Valkyrie*. And nobody escapes from this place. You're going to die." She walked away, but she looked unhappy. The guards pulled Thor away, and tied him to a chair.

An old man came toward him. He lifted a strange machine with many sharp knives on it. "Don't move," he said to Thor. "My hands shake sometimes."

"You will *not* cut my hair ..." Thor shouted. "I am Thor! You cannot—"

The man turned on his machine and the knives cut through the air.

"Please, kind sir, do not cut my hair! No!" Thor said ...

Thousands of people were sitting around the theater, and spaceships were flying above it. Valkyrie's ship was there, too.

Loki was sitting with the Grandmaster in a comfortable room. They were looking down at the crowd of Sakaarians.

The Grandmaster spoke to his people. "*Wow!* Look at all of you. Are you having fun? This is the game that you're here for. It's time for the big fight! For the first time ... meet the Lord of Thunder!"

Thor's hair was very short and his beard was shorter, too. He was dressed for fighting. He walked into the theater and looked up at the screaming crowd.

The Grandmaster shouted, "O.K., now let's welcome the champion! What can I say about him? There's nobody like him. He's the best fighter on Sakaar. Nobody can fight him and win! Here he is ...!"

KA-BOOM! A very big, green man ran through a door into the theater. He hit his chest and screamed loudly.

Thor started to laugh. The Grandmaster's champion was Hulk!

Loki was very worried. He remembered his past fights with Hulk. *I have to escape from this planet,* he thought. He tried to leave the room, but the Grandmaster stopped him.

"Hey! Where are you going?" He pushed Loki into a seat near the window.

In the theater, Thor was still laughing. He pointed at Hulk. "Hey, Banner!" he said. He was using the green man's Earth name.

Thor turned to the crowd. "I know him! He's a friend from work. Banner, you're not dead. I'm so happy to see you! A lot has happened. I lost my hammer. And Loki's alive. Can you believe that? He's up there." He waved to Loki. "Loki! Look who's here!"

Hulk shouted, "I am not *Banner*! I am *Hulk*!"

"Hulk! Hulk! Hulk!" the crowd shouted.

Hulk ran toward Thor.

"What are you doing?" Thor asked. "It's me! I'm really happy that you're here."

He stepped to one side and missed the first attack. But then Hulk caught him and threw him in the air.

Thor pulled out two swords. "Banner, we're friends. This is crazy. I don't want to hurt you!"

Hulk kicked Thor into a wall.

Thor started to fight, and Hulk fell on the floor. "Hey, big guy," Thor said. "I won't hurt you. Nobody will hurt you again."

But Hulk caught Thor's leg, and threw him down onto the floor.

"All right. You *really* want to fight?" Thor asked.

Now they were fighting hard ... and Thor was winning! "I know you're in there, Banner," he said. "I'll get you out! What's your problem? We were friends!"

Hulk jumped on top of Thor and hit the God of Thunder on the head. Then, he threw him against the wall again.

Suddenly, Thor thought about Odin. Lightning shone in his eyes and

they turned white. His arms felt very strong and he hit Hulk hard. Hulk fell back against the theater wall.

The crowd started to shout, "ThunDER! ThunDER! ThunDER!"

The Grandmaster was angry. He didn't want his champion to lose the fight. He pushed his control switch for the metal disk in Thor's neck. Thor dropped to the ground.

Hulk jumped up high into the air. Thor looked up and saw the big, green man coming down toward him. And then, Hulk fell on top of him ...

Hela was sitting on the throne of Asgard. Skurge was standing near her. "What's that noise?" she asked.

"Some Asgardians are trying to knock down the front gates of the palace," Skurge replied.

Hela sent her soldiers to kill them. She and Skurge went to the end of the Rainbow Bridge. "Skurge, where's the sword?" Hela asked, looking around her. "Who took the sword that opens the Bifrost?" She was very angry. "Get those people who are fighting me. Bring them here."

Men, women, and children ran away from Hela and her soldiers, into the woods.

BAM! One family ran into a tall man. It was Heimdall!

Quickly, Heimdall pulled out the Bifrost sword. He killed the soldiers who were following the family. Then, he turned to them. "Follow me," he ordered.

They walked with him into the mountains. Heimdall stopped and opened large doors in the rock. Inside the mountain were hundreds of Asgardians—strong and weak, young and old.

Heimdall smiled at the family. "You'll be safe here," he said.

Suddenly, Thor thought about Odin. Lightning shone in his eyes and they turned white.

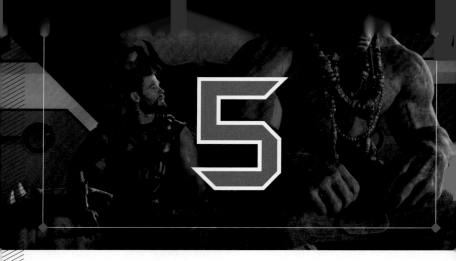

5

The New Team

Thor was lying on the floor in Hulk's apartment. He was very dirty and his body hurt. He heard a noise behind him and turned. Hulk was sitting in a large, hot bath.

"Are we friends?" Thor asked.

"I guess we are," Hulk replied.

"Why are you big, green ... and dumb? What happened to Banner?"

"There *is* no Banner. Hulk is *always* Hulk."

Thor walked to a window. Outside, he saw an old spaceship. It traveled higher and higher, toward a portal in the sky. Then, *BOOM!* One of the Grandmaster's spaceships destroyed it.

Thor looked at Hulk. "How did you travel here?"

"On a spaceship. A Quinjet."

"Where is the Quinjet now?" Thor asked.

Hulk climbed out of the bath. Thor closed his eyes. Hulk wasn't wearing any clothes. *That's a terrible picture*, Thor thought. *It will stay in my head all my life.*

Hulk pointed out the window. Thor looked out and saw the Quinjet, with scrap everywhere around it. "Yes!" he said. Now he could escape. "We're leaving here. We're going to Asgard. You'll love it—it's big, golden, and shiny."

Hulk sat on his bed. "I will stay here."

"My people need me in Asgard. We must stop Ragnarok—the end of everything. We'll go to Asgard, then I'll take you back to Earth."

"People on Earth hate Hulk," the green man said.

"The people on Earth *love* Hulk! We *all* love you—you're our friend. And good friends always help their friends."

"You're *Banner's* friend."

"I'm *not* Banner's friend. He talks about numbers and science all the time. I like *you*."

"*You* can go to Asgard. Hulk is staying here."

"O.K., stay here!" Thor went to the open door. "I'm going." But then the metal disk in his neck stopped him, and he fell to the floor.

Hulk laughed and walked out of the room.

Thor went back to the window. He looked at the sky, then closed his eyes. "Heimdall, I know you're there," he said. "I need your help."

Thor's eyes turned golden when he opened them again. His mind traveled to Asgard and took him to his friend.

Heimdall turned to Thor. "I can see you," he said quietly. "But you are far away."

"What's happening here?" Thor asked.

"Come with me. I will show you." Heimdall ran down the street and Thor followed with his mind. He was afraid for the people of Asgard. There was smoke above the city, and there were soldiers everywhere.

"I'm taking our people into the mountains. It is safe there," Heimdall said. "But if Hela finds us, our only escape is the Bifrost."

"Do you want to leave Asgard?" Thor asked.

"We cannot stay. Hela will kill us all. Now, because she's on Asgard, she is getting more powerful every day. When she leaves Asgard, she will destroy all of the Nine Realms. We need your help."

"I'm trying to return to Asgard. But I don't know where I am," Thor said. More soldiers arrived and Heimdall moved away. "You're on a planet far from Asgard. You can get here through the portal!" he shouted.

He began to fight the soldiers, and Thor disappeared.

Thor was still in Hulk's apartment.

Hulk was looking at him. "Is Thor sad?" he asked.

Thor was playing with the metal disk in his neck. He stood up. "You're so dumb! I'm not sad, I'm angry. I lost my father. I lost my hammer." He kicked a sword across the floor.

"Don't kick things," Hulk said.

"You're not listening to me. You're a really bad friend," Thor said.

"*You're* a bad friend!" Hulk said.

"Do you know what we call you?" Thor asked. "Dumb!"

"We call you *small*!" Hulk shouted. He picked up a big piece of metal and threw it at Thor's head.

"Are you crazy?" Thor shouted.

"Yes," Hulk replied.

"You were right," Thor said angrily. "Earth *does* hate you!"

Hulk sat on his bed. He looked very sad.

Thor felt bad about his words. "I'm sorry. You're not dumb. We don't call you dumb."

Hulk said, "I'm sorry. I get angry. Hulk is always, always angry."

Thor sat next to him and spoke slowly. "I'm sorry that I called you dumb. Hulk, I want you to help me ..."

The next morning, Valkyrie came into the apartment with two of the Sakaarian guards. Hulk was playing with a large ball, throwing it at the wall.

The guards left and Valkyrie ran to Hulk. She smiled. "What's happening?" she asked. "What do you ...?"

Hulk moved, and she saw Thor. Her smile disappeared.

"We must talk," Thor said quickly.

"No," Valkyrie said. "*You* want to talk to *me*. *I* don't want to talk to *you*." She started to leave the room.

Thor turned to Hulk. "I need her to stay."

Hulk picked up part of his bed and threw it across the room. Now Valkyrie couldn't get through the door. "Stay! Please!" he said.

"You must listen to me," Thor said. "Asgard is in danger and people are dying. We must go there—and we need your help."

Valkyrie moved toward the door again.

"Odin is dead," Thor said.

She stopped moving.

"And Hela, the Goddess of Death, has returned," Thor continued.

"If Hela has returned, Asgard is finished," Valkyrie said.

"I'm going to stop her."

"Alone?"

"I'm putting together a team—you, me, and the big guy," Thor told her.

"Hulk is not on the team," Hulk said.

"The team is you and me," Thor said to Valkyrie.

She laughed. "I think it's only you on the team," she said.

"Wait. Listen to me," Thor said. "The Valkyries were the best soldiers in Asgard. It was your job to guard the throne." He moved very close to her and looked into her eyes.

"Your sister is powerful." Valkyrie said. "She was too powerful for Odin. He couldn't control her, and she killed everyone in the palace. She tried to become queen. Odin sent the Valkyries to fight her—*I* fought her. And I lost everything. I lost my friends. Hela killed them. That's the problem with Asgard. It's beautiful on the outside, but it's full of secrets and lies."

Thor put his hand on her shoulder. "I agree with you. That's why I don't want to be king. But this isn't about the crown. This is about the *people*. They're dying—and they're your people, too."

Valkyrie pulled her shoulder away from Thor and pushed him away. "I'm not going to help you."

"O.K.," Thor said. "I understand. But thank you for this."

"For what?"

Thor opened his hand. He was holding the control switch for the metal disk in his neck. "I took this from you. You didn't see that, did you?" He pressed it and the pain in his neck stopped. He pulled off the metal disk. "That's better," he said. "O.K., stay here. Work for the Grandmaster. Hide.

Thor dropped down the side of the Grandmaster's palace onto the street.

But me ... I run *toward* my problems, not *away* from them. Because that's what ..."

Thor took the ball from Hulk and threw it, hard, at the window. He was trying to break it. The ball came back, hit him in the face, and knocked him to the floor.

Thor stood up. "Because that's what brave people do!" he told Valkyrie.

Then he jumped through the glass.

Hulk's voice came after him. "My friend! Stay!"

Thor dropped down the side of the Grandmaster's palace onto the street. He was free! He started running toward the Quinjet.

A few blocks away, Hulk was following him. He ran into people and they fell down. He knocked over vehicles. Nobody was angry, because all the Sakaarians loved their champion.

Thor ran into the Quinjet. "All right. Let's start this spaceship." He pressed the controls.

Hulk ran through the door. He looked very angry. "Stay! Stay, my friend!" he said. He didn't want Thor to leave. He started to destroy the inside of the Quinjet. Thor pressed another control switch, and a woman's face appeared. It was Natasha Romanoff—Black Widow—a woman that Bruce Banner loved. She could calm him when he was angry. Then, he was able to change back from Hulk into Bruce Banner.

Hulk saw her face and moved closer to the computer. He fell onto his hands and knees. He screamed, and his hands pulled at his face. He was shaking his head with pain. He was turning into Bruce Banner.

Thor ran to his side. "Hey, hey. Are you all right, Banner? Move slowly. I won't hurt you."

"Thor?" Banner said. "Where are we? Why are *you* here? And what happened to your hair?"

"An old man cut it off."

"It looks good. Was I Hulk for a long time?"

"Two years."

"I was Hulk for *two years?* Thor, where are we?"

Suddenly, they heard the Grandmaster's voice. "It's bad, bad news today. Sakaarians, listen to me. My wonderful champion has disappeared. Everyone, go onto the streets. The Lord of Thunder has stolen him."

"*God* of Thunder," Thor said angrily.

"Who's that?" Banner asked.

"He's the boss here. You lived in his house."

"I did?" Banner asked.

"A lot has happened. We had a fight."

"Did I win?" Banner asked.

"No, I won easily," Thor replied.

"That doesn't sound right."

"We need to escape," Thor said.

Escape from Sakaar

In the palace, Loki and Valkyrie were standing in front of the Grandmaster.

"I'm unhappy! I'm *very* unhappy," the Grandmaster said. "My champion has disappeared because of the *Lord of Thunder*." He looked at Loki. *"Your brother."* He turned to Valkyrie. "And *you* brought him here!"

"My dear friend," Loki said. "I'll bring them both to you in twelve hours."

"I'll bring them in *two* hours," Valkyrie said quickly.

"I'll bring them in *one* hour!" Loki shouted.

"O.K.," the Grandmaster said. "Let's find the winner."

Valkyrie ran out of the palace and Loki followed her. "What have you done?!" he asked. "You helped my brother escape with that dumb, green champion!"

Valkyrie pushed him into a wall. "You're not my boss, Loki. And I didn't help anyone."

Loki saw the strange, dark picture on the skin of her arm. "You're a Valkyrie," he said slowly. "Didn't all the Valkyries die?"

Valkyrie pulled out her two knives and pressed them against his neck. She wasn't afraid to kill him. "Choose your next words carefully."

"I'm sorry," Loki said. "That was a hard time for you." He put out his hands and touched her head. It was another of his tricks.

Suddenly, Valkyrie remembered her fight with Hela. There was a lot of smoke. People were screaming. The brave soldiers—the Valkyries—fell through dark space and all their horses died. Lots of people were dying—and one of them was Valkyrie's closest friend. Hela killed her.

Angrily, Valkyrie turned to Loki and hit him very hard.

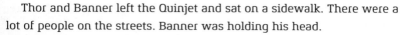

Thor and Banner left the Quinjet and sat on a sidewalk. There were a lot of people on the streets. Banner was holding his head.

"Stay calm," the God of Thunder said.

"*Calm?!*" Banner shouted. "I'm on a strange planet!"

"It's only a planet," Thor said. "You've seen other planets."

"Yes! *One* planet!"

"Now you've seen *two* planets. That's a good thing. It's a new adventure."

"I don't want to become Hulk again. I'm scared that Banner will disappear. I'm afraid that he'll never come back. And we're on a planet that will make me angry. When I'm angry, I become Hulk."

"I'm going to Asgard," Thor explained. "My people are in great danger. You and I must fight a powerful woman—Hela. She's my sister."

"I don't want to fight your sister. That's a family problem."

Suddenly, Valkyrie remembered her fight with Hela.

"She'll destroy Asgard."

"I'm not going to fight anybody. I don't want to be Hulk again."

"I'm putting together a team, and Hulk is an important part of it," Thor said.

"I'm *Banner*. You only want Hulk. You're *his* friend, not my friend."

"No! I don't like Hulk—but he *is* a good fighter," Thor said. "Listen, we're in danger here. Let's move."

Thor saw a group of Scrappers coming toward them. "This is bad," he said.

One of the Scrappers attacked them. Suddenly, Valkyrie was there. *WHAM!* She hit the Scrapper, and he fell to the ground.

Thor looked at her. "Hi. *I* wanted to do that."

"Did you? Well, I did it first. Why are you here? You wanted to leave. And who is this guy?"

"Me? I'm Bruce," Banner said.

"Do I know you?" Valkyrie asked slowly. *I'm sure I know him*, she thought.

"Do *I* know *you*?" Banner asked. *I'm sure I know her*, he thought.

Valkyrie took them into a building. She turned to Thor. "I can't forget my past. I'm going to die one day. I want to kill your murdering sister first. I want to be on the team. And I have a gift for you."

She opened the front door of her apartment. It was a complete mess. There was a knife in the wall. And Loki was tied to a chair in the middle of the room.

"Surprise!" he said to Thor.

Was it the real Loki, or another of his tricks? Thor threw a bottle at

his head.

"*OW!*" Loki shouted. Yes, it was the real Loki.

Loki turned to Banner. "Hello, Bruce."

Valkyrie put an old Asgardian sword on the bed.

"Is that ... a Dragonfang?" Thor asked. "The famous sword of the Valkyrie?"

"It is," Valkyrie said. "But Asgard is a long way from Sakaar. It will take eighteen months to reach it."

"No, we're going through *that* portal," Thor said. He took her to the window and showed her the big, black hole in the sky above the ocean.

"Then we need another spaceship," Valkyrie said. "That portal will destroy my spaceship."

Loki spoke from behind them. "The Grandmaster has many spaceships. And I can get into his garage."

They all turned and looked at him.

"You suddenly want to do the right thing?" Valkyrie asked.

"Oh, no," Loki laughed. "But the Grandmaster doesn't like me now. If you take me away from here, I'll find you a ship."

"There are too many guards at the palace. How can we get past them?" Valkyrie asked.

Loki looked at Banner. "Why not send in the wild animal against them?"

"Be quiet!" Thor said quickly. He looked at Banner, then looked away.

"You guys have a wild animal?" Valkyrie asked.

"No, there's no wild animal. Don't listen to Loki." Thor smiled. "We're going to start a revolution ..."

"No, we're going through *that* portal," Thor said.

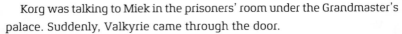

Korg was talking to Miek in the prisoners' room under the Grandmaster's palace. Suddenly, Valkyrie came through the door.

"I'm looking for Korg," she said.

"Who are you?" the rock man asked.

She threw a gun to him. "The Lord of Thunder says hello," she said.

"My revolution has started!" Korg said happily.

Thor and Loki ran into the Grandmaster's palace, and Loki opened a door. Before they could go inside, some Sakaarian guards ran toward them.

"Hello!" Thor said to them.

"Hi!" Loki said at the same time. Then, the brothers lifted up two guns and shot the guards.

The two Asgardians moved toward another door. "We must talk," Thor said.

"Our family is not good at talking," Loki replied. "Odin brought us together. Now he's dead. We're strangers, not brothers. We're not friends. I think I'll stay here on Sakaar. It's a better place for me."

A guard tried to attack Loki, but Thor killed him.

"I think you're right," Thor said.

Loki was surprised. "Are you agreeing with me?"

"This place is perfect for you. It's wild and lawless," Thor replied. "Brother, you're going to do great things here."

"Do you really think I'm a bad person?" Loki asked.

"Loki, I loved you," Thor said. "I wanted to fight at your side for the rest of my life. But we're different. Maybe there *is* still good in you, but we want different things."

Loki was hurt by Thor's words, but he didn't show his feelings. "We won't meet again."

Thor put his arm across Loki's shoulder and held him close. At the same time, he secretly put a metal disk on his brother's back. "That's what you always wanted." Then, he said, "There will be more guards. Let's do 'Get Help.'"

"No!" Loki said. "I hate 'Get Help.'"

"You love it. It works every time," Thor laughed. "Do you have a better plan?"

"We are *not* doing 'Get Help'!" Loki said angrily.

The doors opened into the Grandmaster's garage. It was full of spaceships. A group of Sakaarian guards turned toward them. One of them pointed his gun.

Thor was carrying his brother. "Get help!" he shouted. "Please! My brother is dying. Get help! Help him!" Then, Thor threw Loki at the guards. They all fell down onto the floor.

Loki stood up. "I *hate* 'Get Help,'" he said.

Thor walked toward him. "*I* don't!" he laughed. "Which ship do we take?"

"The *Commodore*."

They went to a beautiful, new spaceship. Suddenly, there were two Lokis—he was playing tricks again. The Loki next to Thor wasn't real.

The real Loki went to a box on the wall. Inside was a switch. "This will bring hundreds of guards to the garage," he said to himself. He turned to Thor. "I've hurt you many times before. But this time it's not because you're my brother. The Grandmaster wants me to catch you. He'll pay me a lot of money for you."

But Thor knew all of Loki's tricks.

Thor pressed the control switch and Loki fell to the ground. Electricity poured through him. Loki was in terrible pain, and he couldn't move.

Thor stood over him. "Oh, brother, you never change. I believe you, then you hurt me." He got down onto his knees. "Loki, life is about change, but you stay the same. You can be a better person, if you choose to be. I'll put this here for you." He placed the control switch on the floor a few meters away. Loki couldn't reach it.

"I have to go. Good luck," Thor said to his brother.

He climbed into the *Commodore*. The garage doors opened and he flew away.

A Race through Space

The Grandmaster and Topaz were inside his big spaceship, the *Statesman*. The *Statesman* formed part of the palace when it wasn't in use.

"There's a revolution?" the Grandmaster said. "How did that happen?"

"I don't know," Topaz said. "But the control disks aren't working. The prisoners are all free. And they have stolen guns."

The *Statesman* broke away from the palace and, with six smaller Sakaarian warships, flew over the city. They had to stop the revolution.

Valkyrie and Banner were in her spaceship, the *Warsong*, when they heard the Grandmaster's voice.

"The Lord of Thunder has stolen my ship and my favorite champion," he shouted. "Sakaarians, find him. Thor cannot leave this planet."

More Sakaarian pilots ran to their spaceships. They followed Thor's spaceship, the *Commodore*, and turned their guns on it. Then—*BOOM!*— Valkyrie arrived in the *Warsong*, and she shot the Sakaarian ships out of the sky.

Valkyrie's voice came over the radio into the *Commodore*. "Open the doors," she told Thor.

She flew her spaceship under the *Commodore* and pressed a switch. Banner's chair lifted up, out of her ship and into Thor's.

A minute later, Banner was standing next to Thor at the controls of the *Commodore*. "Shall we shoot at the Sakaarians?" he asked.

"Yes." Thor spoke into the radio. "Where are the guns on this ship?" he asked Valkyrie.

"There aren't any guns," she replied. "The *Commodore* isn't a warship. The Grandmaster uses it for parties."

Thor and Banner looked around. There were mirrors above their heads, and a dance floor. No, the *Commodore* was *not* a warship!

Gunfire hit the *Warsong*. It was one of the Grandmaster's ships shooting at her! Valkyrie destroyed the attacking ship, but then the *Warsong* exploded and broke into pieces. There was smoke and fire everywhere.

"No!" Thor shouted. There was sadness in his eyes. Was Valkyrie dead?

Then he saw somebody flying through the smoke. *THWACK!* Valkyrie hit the front window of the *Commodore*!

"Come inside!" Thor shouted.

"In a minute!" Valkyrie pulled herself onto the roof of the *Commodore*. She ran along it, then jumped onto the Sakaarian spaceship behind them. She pulled it into pieces with her hands!

"I'll go and help her," Thor said to Banner. "You take the controls."

"I don't know how to fly this spaceship." Banner was very worried.

"You're a smart guy. You passed lots of exams."

"Not exams about spaceships!"

Thor jumped out of the *Commodore* and joined Valkyrie.

Banner looked at the controls. "There's a gun here somewhere," he said. He pressed a switch. Suddenly, there were bright lights inside the ship, and loud dance music and colored smoke. Then, Banner heard the Grandmaster's voice. He was singing, "It's MY BIRTHDAY! It's MY BIRTHDAY!" Yes, the *Commodore* really *was* a party ship!

Thor and Valkyrie destroyed one enemy spaceship after another. They threw the pilot from the last one out into the sky, and sat at the controls.

Soon, they were flying under the *Commodore*. Thor and Valkyrie jumped—and then they were with Banner again.

Minutes later, they were near the portal.

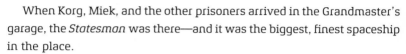

When Korg, Miek, and the other prisoners arrived in the Grandmaster's garage, the *Statesman* was there—and it was the biggest, finest spaceship in the place.

"This ship will take us out of here," Korg said. "Hey, what's this?" Near his feet, he saw a small control switch. He picked it up. Then he noticed Loki lying on the ground.

Korg looked at Loki, then at the control switch, then at Loki again. Suddenly, he understood and pressed the switch. The metal disk in Loki's neck stopped working.

Loki stood up. "Thank you," he said.

"Hey, man, we're going to jump on that big spaceship. Do you want to come, too?" Korg asked.

"Yes—you really need a boss …" Loki said.

The trip through the portal was long and hard. Finally, Thor, Valkyrie, and Banner looked down at Asgard from their spaceship.

"I never wanted to return here," Valkyrie said.

"It's not very nice," Banner said. "It's on fire."

The *Commodore* flew down through the clouds. Asgard *was* on fire. Everywhere, buildings were destroyed, and there were dead soldiers in the streets.

Valkyrie looked at a map on her computer. "There are groups of people up in the mountains. I can see the heat from their bodies on the map."

A crowd of Asgardians was standing together in the middle of the city. Hela's soldiers were standing around them. Skurge was shouting at them. He had a very big sword in his hand.

Hela was behind him, with Fenris, her big wolf.

"Asgardians, somebody has stolen the Bifrost sword," Skurge shouted. "Tell us where it is. If you don't, we will punish you."

The Asgardians were afraid, but nobody spoke.

Hela pointed to a woman. "You."

Her soldiers pulled the woman out of the crowd toward Skurge.

Minutes later, they were near the portal.

"Skurge!" Hela shouted. "Do your job."

"Skurge!" Hela shouted. "Do your job."

Skurge closed his eyes. He didn't want to kill the woman. But he didn't want Hela to kill *him*!

The woman fell onto her hands and knees. Hela looked at Skurge again, and he lifted his sword.

Suddenly, an Asgardian man ran from the crowd. "Wait! I know where the sword is."

Valkyrie was looking at her computer again. She could see everything on Asgard. "Hela is searching for the people in the mountains," she said.

"O.K.," Thor said. "Leave me at the palace and I'll take her away from them."

"No! She'll kill you!" Valkyrie shouted.

"The people down there are more important than me," Thor said. "I'll attack Hela. You and Banner take everyone away from Asgard."

"How can we do that?" Banner asked.

"I have a friend down there," Thor replied. "He'll help you."

Valkyrie landed the *Commodore* on Asgard. She and Thor put a big Asgardian gun into the side of the spaceship. "Now we can fight," Thor said.

Valkyrie climbed into the pilot's seat. She looked at Thor for a long time. "I'll go to the Asgardians," she said. "And, my king, don't die!"

Then she flew away.

Heimdall was taking the Asgardians away from the mountain. "We must move! Go to the Bifrost!"

Hela and Skurge arrived at the other side of the mountain. The Goddess of Death lifted her arms and sent long, thin knives into the rock. She was very strong, and the great doors fell from the mountain. She waited for the air to clear, but Heimdall and the Asgardians weren't there.

Suddenly, Hela heard a loud noise from far away. She looked at the palace. *Thor has arrived*, she said to herself.

In the palace, Thor was sitting on the throne. Hela came into the room and walked toward him. "Sister," he said.

She smiled. "You're still alive," she said.

"I understand why you're angry," Thor said. "I got the throne of Asgard— the job that *you* wanted. Odin told us both lies."

Hela laughed. "Odin was very powerful when he was at his best. He and I killed thousands of people. That is where the gold in the palace came from. And then, one day, he changed. He wanted to be a *good* king. He didn't want any more wars. He wanted a son—you."

"You are my sister and Odin's oldest child," Thor said. "You want to be Queen of Asgard. Believe me, I don't want to be king. But you *can't* be queen. You're too ... scary."

Hela looked bored. "O.K., get up," she said. "You're in my seat."

Thor stood up. "A wise king never wants war. Those were our father's words."

"But a wise king is always *ready* for war," Hela said.

They started to fight.

8

No Place to Run

Heimdall was taking the Asgardians onto the Rainbow Bridge. Suddenly, he stopped. At the far end of the bridge was Fenris! The big wolf was guarding the controls to the Bifrost. The Asgardians couldn't run past it.

Heimdall shouted to his people, "Go back!"

They turned, but Fenris ran toward them. Its mouth was wide open, showing its terrible, sharp teeth.

The Asgardians heard the sound of guns from above them. Valkyrie was shooting at the wolf from the *Commodore*.

But the Asgardians couldn't escape. At the other end of the Rainbow Bridge, Skurge stood in front of hundreds of Hela's soldiers.

"Heimdall!" he shouted. "Give me the Bifrost sword!"

Hela's soldiers ran toward the Asgardians, but Valkyrie and Banner shot at them from their spaceship. There were dead soldiers everywhere. Now there was a path along the bridge for Heimdall and his crowd of Asgardians.

Heimdall looked at the palace. What was happening to Thor? But there was no time to help his friend. The Asgardians were more important. He turned to the people behind him. "Come with me. We must cross the bridge now to the Bifrost!"

Valkyrie shot at Fenris again, but she couldn't kill the animal. The wolf was really angry now, and it ran toward the Asgardians again. Heimdall stepped out in front of them with his sword.

Valkyrie stopped shooting. "I can't kill this stupid dog!" she shouted to Banner.

Banner looked down at the Rainbow Bridge. He—or Hulk—was the only person who could stop the wolf. He stood up and walked to the door of the spaceship. He turned to Valkyrie. "Everything will be O.K. Do you want to know who I am?"

She looked at him. "What are you talking about?"

"You'll see." Banner jumped out of the ship and flew through the air. He was turning into Hulk again ... But nothing happened. *SPLAT!* Banner fell on his face on the bridge.

Fenris walked slowly toward him. The wolf was interested. What was this? Something to eat?

Was Banner finally dead? But then the skin on his neck turned green. He started to grow bigger—and greener. Finally, he was Hulk again!

He hit Fenris hard in the face. They started to fight and they both fell off the bridge into the water below.

Valkyrie flew the *Commodore* to the city side of the bridge. She brought it down near Skurge and the soldiers, then she stepped out of the spaceship. Her sword—her Dragonfang—was in her hand. She smiled when the soldiers ran toward her. She was a Valkyrie. She was ready to fight.

Fenris walked slowly toward him. The wolf was interested.

The Asgardians were standing in a large crowd on the bridge. There were a lot of them and some almost fell into the water below. Their friends reached out to them and pulled them back. But they couldn't escape.

In the palace, Hela and Thor were fighting.

"You and I are different," Hela said. "I'm Odin's first-born child. I will save Asgard. And you are nothing."

She lifted her sword and cut out one of Thor's eyes. "Now you look like Dad," she said happily.

She lifted Thor and held him by his neck. With his one eye, he could see the Rainbow Bridge. "Look down there," Hela said. "Nobody can escape. I will get that sword. I will kill every Asgardian and get it."

Thor looked down at his people on the Rainbow Bridge. *What can I do to save them?* he asked himself.

Heimdall was fighting hard. A soldier knocked him down and stood over him. *I'm going to die*, Heimdall thought.

Then—*BAM!*—the soldier fell down dead.

Korg walked toward Heimdall. He was holding a big gun. "Hey, man," he

"I'm Odin's first-born child. I will save Asgard. And you are nothing."

said. "I'm Korg and this is Miek. We're going to jump back on that spaceship and leave here." He pointed to the *Statesman*. "Do you want to come?"

There was a loud noise. With his arms wide and horns on his head, Loki stood above the Rainbow Bridge! "I've come to save you," he shouted.

He was standing on top of the *Statesman*. The other prisoners from Sakaar were with him—and they all had guns.

The spaceship stopped in the middle of bridge. Loki and his men jumped off and joined the fight against Hela's soldiers.

"Did you miss me?" Loki shouted. "Everybody, get on that spaceship now!" Then, he walked through the crowd to help Heimdall.

"Welcome home," Heimdall said.

The Asgardians ran onto the *Statesman*. Thousands of scared people were trying to escape.

From the palace, Hela and Thor saw Loki on the bridge. "So, he's returned!" Hela said angrily.

Thor smiled when he saw his brother.

Hela turned to Thor. "You were brave, but you can never win. I'm not a queen, I'm the Goddess of Death. What were *you* the god of? I can't remember."

Thor looked at the Rainbow Bridge. His friends were protecting his people. He looked up at the stars. Suddenly, Hela pressed the two knives into his chest. Thor screamed ... and everything went silent.

He opened his eye. He was in a field, and Odin was standing in front of him.

Thor fell to his knees. "Father, she's too powerful," he said. "Without my hammer, Mjolnir, I cannot—"

Odin's voice was strong and loud. "Are you Thor, God of Hammers? No. That hammer helped you, but it didn't give you your power."

Thor looked up at his father. "It's too late," he said. "Hela has already won the fight for Asgard."

"Asgard is not a *place*. It never was," his father said. "It is *people*. Asgard is where our people stand together. And now those people need you."

"I'm not as strong as you," Thor said.

"No," Odin said. "You're stronger."

Odin turned away, and Thor closed his eye. When he opened it again, he was in the palace.

Hela pressed the knives deeper into his chest and he screamed with pain. Above them, the sky was full of black clouds. A storm was coming.

Thor heard Hela's voice. "Tell me again, brother. What were you the god of ...?"

There was a loud noise—it was thunder. Lightning poured through Thor and into his arms. It covered him and Hela!

The lightning hit Hela and she crashed down onto the streets of Asgard. *BOOM!* It pushed Thor to the Rainbow Bridge.

He was very powerful and strong now. He attacked the soldiers and pushed hundreds of them off the bridge. When they came too close to him, he killed them.

Valkyrie ran toward him with her Dragonfang in her hand. She stood next to him and started fighting, too.

In the center of the bridge, Heimdall was pushing the Asgardians into the *Statesman*. Loki, Korg, and the other prisoners from Sakaar were shooting at Hela's soldiers.

"Hela is going to lose this fight," Skurge said to himself. He pulled a piece of cloth over his head. Now nobody could see his face. Then, he quietly left the soldiers and joined the Asgardians.

It pushed Thor to the Rainbow Bridge.

The Last Great Fight
for Asgard

In the water below the bridge, Fenris was holding Hulk in his mouth. Hulk pushed the wolf under the water and hit it on the nose. Then Fenris tried to bite Hulk.

They fought for a long time until they reached the end of the realm of Asgard. Hulk hit Fenris, and the wolf fell away, into space. Hulk tried to climb onto the bridge again, while water poured over him.

Thor and his friends were still fighting the soldiers. Thor saw his brother. "You're late," he said.

Loki laughed. "What happened to your eye?" he asked.

Suddenly, Valkyrie noticed that Hela was at the other end of the bridge. The Goddess of Death was strong. She was ready to kill.

Valkyrie pointed at her and shouted to Thor, "This fight hasn't finished yet!"

Hela walked slowly toward them. Thor, Loki, and Valkyrie stepped toward her to protect the Asgardians.

"Hit her with lightning," Loki suggested to Thor.

"I already hit her with plenty of lightning!" Thor said. "It did nothing."

"We need to fight her until everybody's on the spaceship," Valkyrie said.

Thor looked at the people behind him. "This war won't end. Asgard gives Hela more power. She will come for us. We need to stop her completely."

"So what can we do?" Valkyrie asked.

"I'm not doing 'Get Help,'" Loki said. He looked worried.

Thor saw Hela coming nearer to them. He looked at the palace behind her, and he remembered Odin's words: "Asgard is not a place. It is people." He turned to his brother. "Go and find Surtur's crown."

"That's a brave idea, brother," Loki said. Loki ran to find the crown. Thor and Valkyrie stayed with Hela.

"Shall we fight?" Thor asked Valkyrie.

"You start," Valkyrie replied.

Thor attacked Hela. She had her black knives, but he had the lightning in his body. They fought hard. *Maybe I can win*, Thor thought. But then Hela pushed her knife into his shoulder and ran past him.

Thor ran after her, and Valkyrie followed him.

Above them, the Asgardians were still running up a walkway into the *Statesman*. Suddenly, the *Commodore* spaceship flew below the bridge with Loki at the controls. He was flying toward the palace.

Hela was still fighting Thor and Valkyrie, but she was moving closer and closer to the *Statesman*.

Finally, all the Asgardians were on the spaceship. Heimdall, Korg, and Miek climbed in last.

Thor looked at Heimdall and shouted, "Go! Go now!"

Hela ran to Thor and pushed her knives into him. He fell to the ground.

She lifted her arms. A great, black sword came out of the center of Asgard and into the *Statesman*. Now the *Statesman* couldn't leave Asgard.

The Asgardians were very afraid when Hela's soldiers started climbing from the bridge into the spaceship. In the middle of the crowd was Skurge. He looked around at the Asgardians. *They've done nothing wrong. They cannot die*, he thought.

The first soldiers began to attack a family, but suddenly Skurge was standing in front of them. In his hands were his two guns, Des and Troy. "For Asgard!" he shouted. *POW! POW! POW!* He shot all the soldiers and they fell back, out of the spaceship.

Skurge jumped off the *Statesman* onto the bridge. More soldiers ran toward him and he shot them, too. Behind him, the *Statesman* freed itself from Hela's sword and lifted into the sky.

Hela turned and saw Skurge. He was killing her soldiers with his two big guns and he was moving toward her.

She threw a knife into his heart.

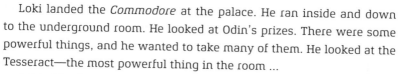

Loki landed the *Commodore* at the palace. He ran inside and down to the underground room. He looked at Odin's prizes. There were some powerful things, and he wanted to take many of them. He looked at the Tesseract—the most powerful thing in the room ...

Loki picked up Surtur's skull, went to the Eternal Flame, and placed the skull into it. "Surtur, you are born again!" he shouted. The fire burned higher, and Surtur's skull grew bigger.

Loki picked up Surtur's skull, went to the Eternal Flame, and placed the skull into it.

Now Hela was fighting Valkyrie—and Hela was winning. She was very angry because the *Statesman* was escaping, above the bridge.

Suddenly, Thor shouted, "Hela! Stop!" He pulled the knife out of his shoulder and put down his sword. "You want Asgard? It's yours."

"I don't believe you. You're playing a game with me. You can't win," Hela said.

"No," Thor said, "but *he* can."

Surtur came through the roof of the palace! He was growing bigger all the time. In the skeleton's hand was a sword covered in flames. The ground under his feet was shaking. There were small holes in the earth, then there were bigger holes. Buildings fell into them. Surtur was destroying Asgard!

Hela was afraid now. "No ... *NO!*" she shouted.

Slowly, the palace started to fall down around Surtur. Above them, the *Statesman* was flying high.

Valkyrie ran toward Hela and pushed her Dragonfang into the Goddess of Death's chest. The sword went through Hela and into the side of the bridge. Now she couldn't move.

Thor ran and pulled Valkyrie away from Hela. He pushed lightning into the Dragonfang, and the lightning broke the bridge under Hela's feet. She fell—and disappeared into a great hole. Was she finally dead?

Thor and Valkyrie looked up and saw Surtur. The skeleton king of Muspelheim was hundreds of meters tall.

"Be afraid, Asgard!" Surtur shouted. He waved his sword and destroyed a city block.

Thor and Valkyrie looked past him at the *Statesman*. "The people are safe," Valkyrie said. "That's more important than the city."

"Ragnarok happened because of us," Thor said sadly.

Behind them, Hulk jumped up onto the bridge, but Thor and Valkyrie didn't see him. He looked around and saw Surtur.

"I destroyed Asgard and Hela. Now my people can live!" Surtur shouted.

Hulk ran at him.

Thor saw his friend. "No! Stop it, you crazy man!"

Hulk jumped onto Surtur's face and hit him. He didn't hurt Surtur, but he did surprise him. Hulk tried to pull off one of Surtur's horns. Surtur picked him up with a big hand of fire and threw him to one side.

Hulk stood up slowly. His skin was burning. Now he was really angry! He moved toward Surtur again.

Thor shouted at him, "Hulk, don't hit him!"

"But he is big! And he is our enemy," Hulk said angrily.

"Hulk! We're leaving," Valkyrie ordered.

Hulk stopped and looked at Surtur, and then at Thor and Valkyrie. He *really* wanted to kill Surtur. But he also wanted to stay with his friends. He turned away from the skeleton king.

Hulk picked up Thor and Valkyrie, and he jumped high into the night sky. He reached the *Statesman,* landed softly on the spaceship, and dropped his friends on the floor.

Down in Asgard, Surtur was destroying everything around him. Suddenly, a great, black knife came out of the water and went into his chest. It came from Hela—she wasn't dead!

Surtur held his sword above his head. "I will destroy Asgard!" he shouted. He pushed his sword through Hela and into the heart of Asgard.

Thor, his friends, and the Asgardians watched from the spaceship.

"It's not too bad," Korg said. "We can build this place again ..."

Surtur's sword was covered with fire. It touched the rocks at the center of Asgard and there was a loud noise. The realm broke into pieces, and Thor's home was completely destroyed. Asgard was gone.

Korg said, "No, sorry. We *can't* build it again."

Down in Asgard, Surtur was destroying everything around him.

"What have I done?" Thor asked sadly.

Heimdall stood next to him. "You saved us. Asgard is not a place. It is people."

An hour later, Thor looked in a mirror. There was a small piece of black cloth over one eye. He looked like his father.

Suddenly, Loki was standing at the door. "That looks good."

Thor smiled. "Maybe *you're* not so bad, brother." He picked up a dish. "But I know you're not really here." He threw the dish. He was surprised when Loki caught it. This *was* his real brother. Loki wasn't trying to trick him.

Loki laughed at his brother and Thor smiled again.

The *Statesman* flew through space and the shining stars. The crowd of Asgardians and Sakaarians in the spaceship waited for their king.

Thor started to walk through them. Many years earlier, when Thor took the crown of Asgard, he was young and proud. Now, he was a different man. Now, he was a kind, serious king.

The people were silent, but they were smiling. They were safe, and they were grateful to Thor.

Hulk, Loki, Valkyrie, and Heimdall were standing next to the pilot's seat. "Here is your throne," Valkyrie said.

Thor sat down.

"So, King of Asgard," Heimdall said. "Where are we going next?"

Thor turned. Hundreds of people were watching him. They were waiting for their king to speak. Slowly, he said, "I'm not sure. Have you any ideas?"

Korg was holding Miek. "Miek, what's your home planet?" Thor asked.

"Oh, Miek's dead," Korg said calmly. "I stepped on him on the bridge—an accident. I feel very bad about that, so I'm carrying him around with me."

Suddenly, Miek started to move.

"Miek! You're alive," Korg said, looking pleased. "Hey, everybody! Miek is alive." He turned to Thor. "What was your question?"

Thor smiled. The rock man was no help. "O.K.—I'll decide. We're going to Earth," he said.

Activities

Chapters 1–2

Before you read

1   Look at the Word List at the back of the book. Check the meanings of new words in your dictionary. Then choose the best words to complete these sentences.

   a The queen sat on a .... and wore a .... on her head.

   b We had a storm. First there was ...., then there was ....

   c The president wants more .... over his people; he is afraid of a ....

   d A .... is a real animal. A .... is not a real animal.

   e She left Earth and flew through a .... to another ....

   f We used .... metal to make new .... and other tools for war.

2   Look at the Who's Who? pages at the front of the book. Then answer these questions.

   a What are the names of Odin's three children?
   b Who wants to destroy Asgard?
   c Who controls the planet Sakaar?
   d Who usually guards the Rainbow Bridge and the Bifrost?
   e Who was one of a group of fighters called the Valkyries?

3   Now read the Introduction, and discuss these questions.

   a Who will return to Asgard after Odin's death?
   b Name two of the Nine Realms.
   c Where is the Eternal Flame? Who wants it?
   d What is Ragnarok?

While you read

4 Circle the right word.

    a Thor is a prisoner on *Earth / Muspelheim*.
    b Surtur wants to destroy *Earth / Asgard*.
    c Thor calls to *a dragon / Heimdall* for help.
    d *Heimdall / Skurge* controls the entrance to the Bifrost now.
    e On Asgard, *Loki / Odin* is watching a play.

5 Put these sentences in the correct order, 1–7.

    a Hela knocks her brothers out of the Bifrost. ....
    b Loki and Thor find Odin. ....
    c Loki disappears into the sidewalk. ....
    d Odin dies. ....
    e Thor and Loki go to New York City. ....
    f Thor and Loki meet Hela. ....
    g Thor meets Doctor Strange. ....

After you read

6 **Work with two or three other students. What have you learned about Thor, Loki, and Hela? Which of these words describe each of them?**

    amusing   angry   bad   brave   crazy   dangerous
    good   loving   proud   smart   strong   weak

Chapters 3–4

Before you read

7 Chapter 3 is called "A Prisoner on Sakaar."

    a What is Sakaar? What do you already know about it?
    b Who will be a prisoner on Sakaar?

While you read

8 Write the speaker's name. Who is the speaker talking to?

a "Are you a fighter, or are you food?"

.... to ....

b "I love your visits, 142."

.... to ....

c "I've never met this man before in my life."

.... to ....

d "Hey! Stay calm, man!"

.... to ....

e "I'll fight him and I'll win."

.... to ....

f "My love!"

.... to ....

9 Use the word *Before* or *After* in these sentences.

a .... the fight, an old man cuts Thor's hair and beard.

b .... Loki sees Hulk, he is very worried.

c .... Hulk starts fighting, Thor calls him "Banner."

d .... Thor thinks about Odin, he becomes very powerful.

e .... the soldiers catch the Asgardian family, they meet Heimdall.

After you read

10 You are Sakaarian. You are at the theater for the fight between Thor and Hulk. What happens? How do you feel at the beginning and end of the fight?

Chapters 5–6

Before you read

11 Discuss these questions.

a Do you think Thor will escape from Sakaar?

b Who will help him?

c Who will be in Thor's new team?

While you read

12 Are these sentences right (✔) or wrong (✗)?

a Hulk came to Sakaar on a Quinjet. ○
b Hulk and Banner are two different people. ○
c The people on Asgard must escape through the Bifrost. ○
d In the past, Valkyrie fought Hela and lost. ○
e Thor thinks he will have to be King of Asgard now. ○
f The Grandmaster wants to find Thor and Hulk. ○

13 Complete each sentence with words on the right. Draw lines between them.

a A Valkyrie is   a spaceship.
b A Dragonfang is   a trick that Loki and Thor play.
c "Get Help!" is   a sword.
d The *Commodore* is   a female soldier.

After you read

14 Work with another student. Have these conversations.

a *Student A*: You are Valkyrie. Tell Thor why you cannot help him against Hela.
Student B: You are Thor. Tell Valkyrie why she must help you.
b *Student B:* You are Banner. Tell Thor why you don't want to help him against Hela.
Student A: You are Thor. Tell Banner why he must help you.

Chapters 7-8

Before you read

15 Discuss these questions. Give reasons for your answers.

a The Grandmaster has lost his champion and the *Commodore*. What will he do next?
b Loki has a metal disk in his neck and he cannot move. What will he do next?

While you read

16 Circle the incorrect word in each sentence. Write the correct word.

  a The prisoners have died. ....

  b Valkyrie's spaceship is the *Commodore*. ....

  c The *Commodore* is a fighting ship. ....

  d Korg leaves Sakaar without Loki. ....

  e A woman tells Hela where the Bifrost sword is. ....

  f The Asgardians leave the mountain after Hela arrives.

  ....

  g Hela finds Thor in the mountain.

  ....

17 Which of these can Hela use in her fight? Check (✔) them.

  a Fenris ◯   **b** Hulk ◯

  c a Dragonfang ◯   **d** a sword ◯

  e the Sakaarian prisoners ◯   **f** knives ◯

  g lightning ◯

After you read

18 Answer these questions.

  a Why must the Asgardians cross the Rainbow Bridge?

  b Why must Banner become Hulk again?

  c Why does Thor look like his father?

  d Why does Skurge join the Asgardians?

Chapter 9

Before you read

19 How do you think this story will end for Hela, Skurge, Thor, and Hulk? Make notes.

While you read

20 Put these sentences in the correct order, 1–8.

a Loki starts Ragnarok. ....

b The Asgardians leave their planet. ....

c Hela dies. ....

d Asgard breaks into pieces. ....

e Thor is hurt. ....

f Hela disappears into a hole. ....

g Hulk attacks Surtur. ....

h Skurge fights for the Asgardians. ....

After you read

21 Work with a partner. Describe what happened to Hela, Skurge, Thor, and Hulk in the final chapter. Then look at your notes from Activity 19. Were you correct?

Writing

22 Choose your favorite part of this book. Write about it. Describe what happens. Say why you like it.

23 You are Odin. You are in Norway, and you are dying. Write a letter to Thor and Loki. Tell them about Hela and Ragnarok. What can they do to protect Asgard? Describe your feelings for your sons.

24 You are a Sakaarian news reporter. Write a report about the fight between Thor and the Grandmaster's champion. Describe what happened between the two fighters. Describe the crowd that was watching the fight. Who did they want to win? Why?

25 You are Valkyrie. What happened after you joined the Valkyries? What happened to you and your friends on Asgard? What happened after you left Asgard? Why did you stay on Sakaar? What did you think of Thor? Why did you join his team? Write your story.

26 You are the Grandmaster. Thor has taken your champion and your spaceship. Write a notice for all Sakaarians to read. Tell them to find Thor, Hulk, and the *Commodore*. Describe them. What should Sakaarians do when they find them?

27 Plan a talk about this book. Introduce the story and the people in it. What are the most exciting parts? What will other readers enjoy? Are there any parts of the book that you didn't enjoy?

28 Thor and Odin are gods in old stories from northern European countries. Are there old stories about gods, or people with special powers, in your country? Write one of the stories.

29 You are interviewing your favorite person from this book for a television show. Write five questions. Then, give your questions to a partner to answer.

Word List

champion (n) the winner of a number of games or fights. A sports champion is the best at his or her sport.

control (n/v) a part of a machine. You press it, or turn it, and the machine works. You can also have control over people, places, or things. They will do what you want.

crown (n) a circle of metal—often gold—worn by kings and queens on their heads on special days. In this book, unusually, Surtur's crown is made of *horns*.

dragon (n) a large animal, in stories, that can fly. Dragons have thick skin and long tails, and they can shoot fire from their mouths.

eternal (adj) continuing or living forever

flame (n) a hot, bright burning gas from a fire. An **eternal flame** is a flame that never goes out.

glove (n) a covering that protects your hand from the cold or in fights

god, goddess (n) someone with *powers* that are more than natural. Many people believe that one or more gods *control* their lives, or a part of life.

hammer (n) a tool, usually with a heavy metal part on a long piece of wood, used for hitting things

horn (n) the hard, pointed part that grows from the heads of some animals

lightning (n) a sudden, bright light in the sky that is produced by electricity during a storm

lord (n) the title of a man who is important, but less important than a king

planet (n) a very large, round body of rock or gas that moves around the sun or another star

portal (n) a large entrance to another place

power (n) the ability—sometimes unnatural—to do something. With power, you can also *control* other people or things. A **powerful** person is very strong or important.

rainbow (n) a half-circle of colors in the sky when there is sun and rain at the same time

realm (n) a country with a king or a queen

revolution (n) a fight to change the government of a country

scrap (n) materials that are not wanted. The materials, or parts of them, can be used for another purpose.

skeleton (n) the hard parts inside the body of a person or animal that give shape to it

skull (n) the hard parts inside a person's or animal's head that give shape to it

sword (n) a long, pointed knife used for fighting

throne (n) a special chair that a king or a queen uses on important days

thunder (n) a sudden, loud noise from the sky during a storm

wolf (n) a wild animal that looks like a large dog